Simple Solutions™

Grooming

By
Kim Campbell Thornton
Illustrations by Buck Jones

With
Practical
Care Tips

BOWTIE
P R E S S ®

A Division of BowTie, Inc.
Irvine, California

Karla Austin, *Business Operations Manager*
Nick Clemente, *Special Consultant*
Kendra Strey, *Project Editor*
Susan Chaney, *Consulting Editor*

Jill Dupont, *Production*
Allyn A. Salmond, *Design*
Michael V. Capozzi, *Cover and book design concept*

The dogs in this book are referred to as *he* and *she* in alternating chapters.

Library of Congress-in-Publication Data
Thornton, Kim Campbell.
   Grooming / by Kim Campbell Thornton ; illustrations by Buck Jones.
     p. cm—(Simple solutions)
   ISBN 1-931993-73-4
   1. Dog—Grooming.   I. Title. II. Series: Simple solutions (Irvine, Calif.)

  SF427.5.T56 2005
  636.7'0833--dc22

2005025739

BowTie Press®
A Division of BowTie, Inc.
3 Burroughs
Irvine, California 92618

Printed and bound in Singapore
10 9 8 7 6 5 4 3 2 1

Contents

Why Grooming Is Great

If you enjoyed playing hairdresser as a kid, you probably love grooming your dog. You're the type of person who should own a coated breed such as a poodle, an Afghan hound, a shih tzu, or one of the many terrier breeds. The rest of us, however, need a little guidance in the ways and means of dog grooming—whether you live with a short-haired, heavy shedder such as a Labrador retriever or a German shepherd dog, or with a fuzzy friend such as a bichon frise or a Havanese.

In this book, you'll learn all the basics of how to keep your dog looking clean, smelling fresh, and feeling good. In addition to these benefits, establishing good grooming habits can help you keep your dog healthy and parasite free. A regular grooming routine gives you hands-on knowledge of your dog's body and is one of the best ways for you to keep tabs on her physical health. When you groom your dog, you're taking a close look at her ears, eyes, mouth, and coat—all of which give you clues to her general health. Regularly grooming your dog may help you discover canine health problems when they're

still easily treatable. Use grooming time to check for lumps, bumps, scabs, or other skin problems; to examine teeth for tartar buildup; and to check eyes and ears for signs of irritation and infection.

Best of all, grooming is a way to spend quality time with your canine best friend. When done correctly, grooming is pleasurable for your dog. Just think how nice it feels when you get a massage or have someone brush out and style your hair. It's the same for your dog. So introduce her to grooming when she's a puppy, and show her how enjoyable it can be. You'll both come to look forward to this relaxing time together.

Coat Types and Shedding

One of the wonderful things about dogs is that they come in a variety of shapes, sizes, and yes, coat types. Some have curly or corded (think dreadlocks) coats, such as those of the poodle and the komondor. Others have long, silky coats, such as those of the Afghan hound and Yorkshire terrier. Medium-length coats are worn by breeds such as the golden retriever and papillon, and short coats by the dalmatian and Labrador retriever. The terrier breeds sport hard coats, at least when kept properly stripped and styled. Spitz breeds such as the Akita, chow chow, and Siberian husky have thick, dense coats.

The amount of grooming your dog requires depends on his coat type. Corded, curly, long, and hard coats all need a fair amount of maintenance if they're going to look their best. For instance, corded coats are prone to matting next to the skin; curly coats must be clipped and shaped; long coats need regular detangling; and hard coats must be hand-stripped (the dead hairs pulled out) instead of clipped or they'll lose their characteristic texture. Shorthaired dogs and those with thick, dense coats need regular brushing and combing because they shed like there's no tomorrow.

Don't think you can escape grooming by acquiring a hairless breed such as a Chinese crested. These dogs have delicate skin that's prone to acne and needs regular moisturizing and sunscreen. You can use coat oil specially formulated for dogs or a gentle moisturizer or baby oil made for human skin, but be sure the product is nontoxic.

Is there a breed that doesn't shed? Not really. All dogs (and people) shed hair on a regular basis; it's part of the hair's growth cycle. The hair of some breeds—the poodle, for example—has a long growth cycle, so it may seem as if they don't shed. However, if you went without vacuuming

for a while, you would eventually find poodle dust-puppies hiding beneath your bed.

Regular brushing is a key to a healthy, shiny coat because it distributes protective skin oils throughout the coat and removes dead hair and dirt. Don't just skim the surface—brush all the way down to the skin to remove dead hair at the source before it falls off the dog and floats onto your clothing, furniture, and floors. By spending just a few minutes a day brushing your dog, you'll spend less time vacuuming the carpet and running a tape roller or lint brush over over your clothes and sofa.

The Goods on Grooming Tools

The amount and type of grooming equipment you need depend on your dog's coat type, and choosing the correct brush will enhance your efforts. A greyhound, with her fine, short hair, needs only a fine-toothed comb, a hound glove, and a bristle brush. On the other paw, maintaining a cairn terrier's rough coat requires a stripping knife, scissors, a stiff bristle brush, and a comb with fine and coarse teeth. Add these tools to the supplies every

dog needs: a toothbrush, dog toothpaste, pet shampoo, and nail clippers; these essentials are discussed in later chapters.

Most brushes come in small, medium, and large sizes, allowing you to choose one that's appropriate for your dog's size as well as for the size of your hand. High-quality tools may carry a heftier price tag than mid-range versions do, but their sturdiness and comfort are worth the price. The following descriptions, as well as advice from your breeder or professional groomer, will help you select the tools that are right for your dog.

A **bristle brush** is what many people use on their own hair. For dogs, a stiff bristle brush removes loose hair and dirt before bathing, whereas a soft bristle brush polishes the coat after a bath and blow-dry. These brushes come with either nylon or natural bristles (brushes with nylon bristles are generally less expensive, but they are stiffer than those with natural bristles and thus may be harsher on the hair). Bristle brushes made specifically for dogs are available in pet supply stores and in most drugstores and grocery stores.

A **hound glove** or hound mitt (sometimes called a curry brush) fits over your hand and has knobby rubber bristles on its palm that lift out dead hair. This tool is best used on short-coated hounds as well as other shorthaired, heavy-shedding breeds such as Labrador retrievers.

A **pin brush** has wire pins—without the sharp tips, of course—set into the pad. This type  of brush helps remove tangles and is especially useful on dogs with long hair or feathering on the legs, body, and tail. A pin brush can also be used to loosen and fluff the dense coats of breeds such as Old English sheepdogs, Pomeranians,

Samoyeds, and Lhasa apsos. Your dog's coat may require a pin brush *and* a bristle brush; if so, look for a double-sided brush with pins on one side and bristles on the other.

A **slicker brush** has curved wire pins that are good for removing mats, dead hair, and debris that your dog's coat picks up. This brush is great for dogs with thick coats, but thin-skinned dogs such as whippets or greyhounds may find it painful if used with too much pressure. (If this is the case, use a hound glove instead.) Avoid using a slicker brush on breeds with fine, silky, straight coats, such as the Yorkshire terrier, because it will damage their hair.

A **chamois cloth** helps remove dust from your dog's coat, which brings out the shine. This tool works wonders on dogs with short, glossy coats, such as the dalmatian,

Doberman pinscher, smooth-coat Chihuahua, and Chesapeake Bay retriever, or on any of the smooth-coated hound breeds. A chamois is useful on any breed for removing excess moisture after a bath. Breeds such as Italian greyhounds and French bulldogs benefit from rub-downs with a velvet glove or silk cloth (varieties of the chamois) to bring out the shine in their coats.

Combs are essential for working through tangles and removing dead hair—left even after a thorough brushing. Combs can have fine, medium, or wide teeth; some ver-sions have two different widths—fine teeth on one half and medium teeth on the other half. Choose a wide-toothed comb if you have a dog with a thick, dense coat, such as a collie, Great Pyrenees, Newfoundland, or

keeshond. High-quality combs are typically made of stain-less steel, although some wide-toothed varieties are made of wood. Combs with very fine teeth are useful for removing fleas.

Some breeds require specialized grooming tools such as **stripping knives**, **stripping stones**, and **thinning shears**. For example, terriers have hard coats that must be hand-stripped (not clipped) if they are to maintain their characteristic texture. Owners who wish to keep their terriers' coats in top condition can apprentice with a breeder to learn how it's done. If that sounds like too much work, or if you don't mind your terrier having a soft coat, have her clipped by a groomer, or learn to clip her yourself.

The type of shampoo and conditioner you use on your dog will also affect the look and feel of her coat. Mild shampoos specifically formulated for pets typically produce the best results. Conditioner keeps your dog's coat shiny and protects her hair from damage caused by grooming. In the next chapter, you'll find tips on choosing the right product types for your dog as well as advice on how to bathe her correctly.

Giving a Bath

If introduced to bathing at an early age, most dogs will tolerate baths, although they might do so grudgingly. Some dogs, however, enjoy bath time so much that you'd think they were at a high-end spa or maybe a water park! Whatever the case, baths are important for keeping your dog's skin healthy, his coat looking well kept, and his body smelling clean.

Frequency of bathing depends on how sensitive your nose is, how sensitive you are about the cleanliness of

your dog if he jumps on the furniture, how well you brush him, and how dirty he gets. For example, if your dog spends a lot of time on your furniture, you may want to wash him weekly with a mild shampoo. Most dogs, however, are bathed only as needed, which is usually only once or twice a year. Breeds such as retrievers and water spaniels should be bathed as infrequently as possible so their naturally oily coats remain water-repellent.

What about hairless dogs? Do they need baths? Well, it depends on the dog. If he has nice skin with small pores, you probably don't need to bathe him unless he gets dirty.

Some hairless dogs have oily skin or acne, so they may need a bath with mild shampoo once every week or two. (These dogs may benefit from a medicated shampoo or acne medication prescribed by a veterinarian.) Facial cleansing cloths made for humans, such as those from Oil of Olay and Neutrogena, are a good way to clean a hairless dog. Baby wipes work, too, and may be a less expensive option.

There are just about as many kinds of shampoos for dogs as there are for people. You can find color-enhancing shampoos, such as those formulated for dogs with white coats, colloidal oatmeal shampoos for dogs with dry skin, medicated shampoos for dogs with acne and other skin problems, and shampoos with designer fragrances. Make sure the shampoo you choose does not contain sodium lauryl sulfate, which can irritate canine skin. For the average dog, a mild canine shampoo will be fine. (A dog's skin has a different pH level than human skin has, so shampoos made for people can be too harsh.) If your dog has a high-maintenance curly, corded, dense, or hard coat, ask a breeder to recommend an appropriate shampoo.

Conditioner leaves the coat shiny, moisturizes the hair, helps prevent hair breakage during grooming, and can even repel dirt between baths. Many conditioners are applied after shampooing and then rinsed out. You might prefer to use a spray-on, leave-in conditioner, which you apply after the bath, before blow-drying.

The ideal place to bathe any size dog is in a large walk-in shower with a seat and a handheld shower nozzle. If you have a big dog, sit on the seat while you bathe him. If you have small dog, place him on the seat so you don't have to bend over too much to reach him.

A kitchen sink with a spray nozzle also makes a great tub for small dogs. Labs, goldens, or other water-loving dogs may enjoy being bathed outdoors on a warm, sunny day. Do this on a concrete or other hard surface—standing in muddy grass will defeat the purpose of the bath.

The secret to a successful dog-bathing experience is organization. Prepare the bathing area so you have towels, a comb, shampoo, and conditioner at hand. Place a nonskid mat in the bathing area, and then go get your dog. (If your dog doesn't like baths, never call

him to you and then plop him in the tub; he'll simply learn that coming when you call is a bad idea.) Before you wet him down, brush and comb him to remove all tangles—they just get worse if they're wet. Dab mineral oil around his eyes to prevent soapy water from running into them.

Using warm water (which helps open the pores and loosen dry, dead hair), wet him down to the skin, starting at the back of his neck and working your way to the tail. Avoid wetting the top of the head and face; you don't want soapy water running into his eyes and ears. Instead, use a damp washcloth or sponge to clean the face and top of the head. If this is his first bath or if he tends to be sensitive to noises, hold the nozzle close to the coat so he's not frightened by the sound of the spray. Apply shampoo and massage it in slowly and thoroughly. If you find any tangles that you had missed, apply a little conditioner to them and gently work them out with your fingers or with the comb.

Squeeze his paw or tail to see if the water runs clean. If it looks dirty, add a little more water and continue massaging the shampoo into the hair. When the soapy water coming off your dog looks clean, it's time to rinse. Rinse until you're sure all the shampoo is gone; then, rinse some more—soap residue will leave your dog with dry, itchy skin, so take the extra time to ensure that all the soap is gone. You may want to follow up with a rinse of a 50:50 mixture of apple cider vinegar and water. In addition to keeping the coat shiny, vinegar helps cut through and remove remaining soap. According to an old wives' tale, vinegar may also help repel fleas, so it doesn't hurt to try it.

Follow the vinegar rinse with a liquid conditioner; apply it and then rinse it thoroughly. Squeeze as much water as you can from your dog's coat before moving on to the drying stage.

Towel dry your dog and let him shake. Then, continue towel drying. (You might want to purchase a superabsorbent sports towel.) The more your dog shakes, the less time you'll have to spend drying him, so let him shake away. Some dogs learn to shake on command, so reinforce the behavior with "Good shake!"

If you chose a spray-on, leave-in conditioner in lieu of a liquid conditioner, spritz the product onto your dog's coat once he's damp-dry.

Finish the job with a blow-dryer. Breeders and grooming professionals usually use powerful stand or cage dryers, which you may want to invest in if you have a large, furry dog or if you'll be washing multiple dogs. To prevent discomfort or burns, set the blow-dryer on medium or cool, and hold it at least six inches away from your dog's body.

Start at the ears and work your way back. With a brush in

one hand (use a pin brush on longhaired dogs and a bristle

brush on shorthaired dogs) and the dryer in the other, go through the coat until it's dry all the way down to the skin. Brushing while blow-drying also helps remove dead hair.

Though not recommended, if you allow your dog to air dry, you must keep him in a warm, draft-free area to prevent chills. If not dried thoroughly, some dogs can develop hot spots (painful, swollen patches on the skin that may require that your dog be sedated or anesthetized to clean the area). A common cause of hot spots is dead, matted hair trapped next to the skin—the extra brushing your dog gets when you blow-dry him will help prevent him from developing these sores.

Doggy Dental Hygiene

If you've been relying on a rawhide chew and a diet of dry food to keep your dog's teeth clean and her breath sweet, think again. If you ate turkey jerky and dry cereal every day and didn't brush your teeth, nobody—not even your dog—would want to come near you.

Daily brushing is the most important thing you can do to keep your dog's breath fresh and her teeth tartar free. Good dental hygiene can also increase her life span. Regular brushing helps prevent bacteria from building up beneath the gum line where they can enter the bloodstream and settle in the heart valves, kidneys, and liver and cause damage to the organs. This is espe-

cially serious in senior dogs or dogs with an otherwise compromised immune system.

Introduce your dog to teeth brushing when she's a puppy. Getting her accustomed to the routine as a pup will save you from having to wrestle her when she's older and bigger. Use a brush with soft bristles and lots of fibers. A child's toothbrush is

fine, or you can purchase a toothbrush made specifically for dogs. The toothpaste you use should be specially formulated for pets; toothpaste made for humans contains detergents that can upset a dog's stomach. Brushing your dog's teeth can be awkward, but as long as you brush the fronts of the teeth as well as the molars, you'll be ahead of the game.

If your dog is reluctant to have her teeth brushed, start by brushing just a few teeth at a time. Praise her while you're brushing, and offer her a tartar-control treat after you're finished. She'll soon look forward to having her teeth brushed.

There are lots of new products that help keep your dog's mouth healthy along with regular brushing. Kibble and treats coated

with plaque-busting substances and tartar-control rinses, gels, and wipes can take a bite out of periodontal disease. One new product that helps prevent plaque from forming on teeth is Oravet, a waxy barrier that's applied by the veterinarian

during a professional cleaning. The pet owner follows up with weekly applications at home, spreading the gel on the dog's gums with a finger or an applicator stick. These weekly applications throughout the dog's life can increase the amount of time needed between professional teeth cleanings.

Sprays, rinses, and wipes containing chlorhexidine or zinc ascorbate cysteine (ZAC) compounds are available from your veterinarian. Chlorhexidine products contain enzymes that dissolve plaque and help reduce bacteria. ZAC compounds encourage collagen production, which helps stimulate the repair of gum tissue. There are a variety of tartar-control chews coated with chlorhexidine, hexametaphosphate, or enzymes that fight plaque. Of course, none of these foods or other products takes the place of brushing—but they're better than nothing!

Although these products help control the buildup of plaque and tartar, they do not treat periodontal disease. If your dog has developed periodontal disease—most dogs who develop the disease do so by four years of age—a veterinary cleaning under anesthesia and subsequent periodontal disease treatments can keep it from advancing. Your veterinarian may recommend placing chips or gels containing antibiotics beneath the gum line. The antibiotics help stop the disease's progression and may restore some of the bone lost from receding gums.

What about flossing? Encourage your dog to chew on rope or sheepskin toys, or give her a Dental Kong chew toy, which has special grooves designed to clean teeth and gums. (Fill the grooves with doggy toothpaste for extra cleaning power.) Give her raw baby carrots and apple slices as treats—they're good for her teeth, too.

Monthly (at the very least), check your dog's mouth for signs of infection such as redness, loose teeth, or other areas that appear to be painful. Do the sniff test: bad breath isn't normal.

Routine Care from Ears to Toes

In addition to keeping your dog bathed and brushed, you'll need to give him the same kind of routine grooming care that you'd give yourself: clean the goop out of his eyes, wipe dirt and excess wax from his ears, and trim his nails. Wrinkly breeds such as basset hounds, bloodhounds, bulldogs, Chinese shar-pei, and pugs must have their wrinkles kept clean and dry to prevent smelly infections.

To care for your dog's eyes, use a damp washcloth to wipe away mucus that accumulates in the corners of his eyes. Some dogs tend to tear excessively—common among bichons frises, poodles, various spaniel breeds, and flat-faced breeds—and have resulting ugly stains beneath the eyes. Excessive tearing can also be a sign of problems such as allergies, blocked tear ducts, or eyelash abnormalities. Your veterinarian will determine the cause of the tearing, which is usually treatable with medication or surgery. Whatever the cause, to prevent or reduce stains from tearing, clean beneath the eyes frequently—which can mean several times a day—using a damp washcloth and mild shampoo. Apply petroleum jelly or a commercial tear stain remover beneath the eyes to prevent tears from penetrating the fur and causing stains.

Healthy ears require little care. Give your dog's ears a good sniff every week to make sure they don't smell bad. An odor typically indicates an infection. A light coating of wax in the ears is normal, but heavy deposits of wax or dirty-looking wax can indicate a problem. Wipe out ears as needed with a cotton ball moistened with mineral

oil or a gentle commercial ear cleaner. Avoid cleansers that are alcohol based; they not only dry out the ear but also can sting if the ear has a sore spot. Be sure to clean only the visible part of the ear—never stick a cotton swab down the ear canal because you could push dirt farther into the ear or puncture the eardrum.

Click, click, click. No, that sound isn't Santa's reindeer; it's your dog's nails hitting the floor—a reminder that they need to be trimmed. Keeping the nails short helps your dog walk properly and prevents accidents such as tearing (as can happen to long nails that get caught in carpet). Trimming your pup's nails also saves your legs from getting scratched if he jumps on you.

Nails should be even with the paw pad, so trim anything longer than that (if it's been longer than a month since your dog's last trimming, clip a little each week or so until you reach the proper length). Use nail clippers designed for dogs (available at pet supply stores). Typically, they have a ring that's placed over the dog's nail and a sharp blade that moves up and cuts when the handle is squeezed. It's always a good idea to have a helper so one of you can hold the dog while the other clips the nails.

The most important thing to remember when clipping nails is not to hit the quick (a collection of blood vessels and nerves inside the nails). Hitting that spot is painful to the dog and results in lots of spurting blood. Be prepared to stop the bleeding with styptic powder if you make a mistake. It's easy to see the quick on dogs with light-colored nails because it appears as a dark line down the middle of the nail, ending before the nail starts to curve

under. To avoid hitting the quick, look for this line and clip below it. For a dog with dark nails, it's more of a guessing game. If you're worried about hitting the quick, trim just a little bit each day until the nails reach the proper length. Any time you see a black dot in the center of the nail, stop! That's the quick.

If the canine love of your life is a wrinkly breed, he'll need special care. Keeping wrinkles clean and dry helps prevent irritation and infection. Once a week, clean between the

wrinkles using a damp washcloth. At bath time, thoroughly rinse off the shampoo—triple check between the wrinkles! After cleansing, thoroughly dry the coat and dust it with cornstarch or baby powder, being sure to get between the wrinkles (the powder will absorb any remaining moisture).

The beard, mustache, and Groucho Marx–like eyebrows of breeds such as the bearded collie and the schnauzers and terriers are known as furnishings and require extra care as well. Frequently wash your dog's furnishings to remove bits of food and other debris. Thoroughly dry your dog's face after he drinks. Give food and water in stainless steel dishes rather than in plastic or crockery dishes, which can discolor the beard.

Regular, thorough grooming is one of the best and most inexpensive ways to keep tabs on your dog's physical condition. The bonus is that you have a clean, beautiful dog you can show off with pride.

Kim Campbell Thornton is an award-winning writer and editor. During her tenure as editor of *Dog Fancy*, the magazine won three Dog Writers Association of America Maxwell Awards for best all-breed magazine. Her book *Why Do Cats Do That?* was named best behavior book in 1997 by the Cat Writers Association. Kim is the author of the Simple Solutions™ series books *Barking*, *Chewing*, *Digging*, *House-Training*, and *Aggression*. She is also the former president of the Cat Writers Association.

Buck Jones' humorous illustrations have appeared in numerous magazines (including *Dog Fancy* and *Cat Fancy*) and books. He is the illustrator for the best-selling Simple Solutions™ series as well as *Why Do Cockatiels Do That? Why Do Parakeets Do That? Kittens! Why Do They Do What They Do?* and *Puppies! Why Do They Do What They Do?* You can contact Buck through his Web site, http://www.buckjonesillustrator.com.